SPIRITUAL

FREEDOM

2018

Dr Rudi

SPIRITUAL FREEDOM 2018

Author: Dr Rudolph Niemand Publisher: Amazon Createspace

TABLE OF CONTENTS

INTRODUCTION

Freedom is something we all desire. It is healthy for us to feel at peace and free.

Anything that disturbs peace and freedom causes us to be out of balance.

Many of us can only handle so much on a daily basis, and anything more make us feel out of control.

Peace with our self, the world, and family are daily dynamics that can be difficult to maintain.

What if there is a spiritual world that we are unaware of that comes against the Prince of Peace?

The Prince of Peace was killed at the age of 33 years.

He is your Prince of Peace and His truth will restore your soul.

Now the Kingdom of Light and the Kingdom of Darkness are at war. The Kingdom of light advances by truth that enlightens you so that the chains of darkness fall off.

This book has many practical points to see the spiritual world and freedom that is available.

CHAPTER 1

WHAT IS A SPIRIT?

Jesus says God is Spirit. The words **breath, air, and wind** in the Hebrew and Greek languages indicated that spirit is just that.

Practical points

So, when you **declare freedom** over an oppressed (sick/diseased) person, you may notice them coughing. The "bad breath" is leaving. The evil spirit is leaving.

Now spirits can leave by yawning, crying, screaming, vomiting, urination, bowel movement, and sudden menstruation.

Spirits manifest their nature. Jesus reveals that in John 10:10. **Foundational Truth** – you need to understand you work with spirits.

John 10:10

"The thief does not come except to steal, and to **kill,** and to destroy. I have come that they may have **life**, and that they may have it more abundantly."

CHAPTER 2

YOU NEED A PLATFORM

Many people that are oppressed by spirits and tormented with pain; anxiety; fear; depression etc. need someone with the knowledge and experience to help them.

People will go to a plumber for a plumbing problem. If there was crime they will go to the police.

So will people know that you are helping with spiritual problems. Everyone has their expertise and experience.

Practical points

- When people know that you help with **spiritual oppression,** they will come to you for spiritual freedom.

- This will provide for you a **platform for ministry** to help those in need. People want their freedom and come from far away.   Our platform is Thursday nights here in Sylvan Lake at our Local Healing and Deliverance Rooms since 2014.

CHAPTER 3

GIVE YOUR PLATFORM A NAME

You can call it Healing Rooms. Keep in mind what you call it and bring an expectation of service.

Practical Points

We call ours **Healing and Deliverance Rooms.** This describes that they are coming for healing and the casting out of unclean spirits.

It also helps people not to come in with an attitude of pride. People get their freedom quicker if they deal with pride themselves.

James 4:6-7

'But He gives more grace. Therefore He says: God resists the proud, But gives **grace to the humble.** Therefore submit to God. **Resist** the devil and he will **flee** from you.'

Practical Points

- Pride is in our flesh and is very much Satan's main nature. When people humble themselves under the Word and the Holy Spirit, freedom and blessing become easy.

CHAPTER 4

SPIRITS AMPLIFY EMOTIONS

We all have emotions, and emotions are healthy and beautiful. With emotions, we can express how we feel.

We laugh out loud to show we are happy or cry when we are unhappy. Our emotions help us to communicate.

Practical Points

- Spirits can **amplify our emotions, enslave us, keep us in bondage**, and manipulate us.

- Spirits of anxiety **can control us** and others around us. Anxiety makes us believe we are sick by confusing our mind with a racing heart, fast breathing, sweating, sleepless nights, and fear of a bad outcome. It is an illusion, a spirit making us think of death and even make us fear death.

2 Timothy 1:7

"For God has not given us a **spirit** of fear, but of **power** and of love and of a sound mind."

CHAPTER 5

AMPLIFIED ANXIETY

People with anxiety have some things in common: They **control their way of living** and circumstances. They **feel quickly overwhelmed** if certain things get out of control. This causes their anxiety to worsen.

It seems like **control** gives them a sense of security that in somehow, they can prevent a bad outcome or even predict the next thing to expect.

Controlling their weight seems to give them some satisfaction. Excessive exercises help to lower or control their anxiety. Obsessive traits lead to physical damage to ligaments, joints etc.

Anxiety is also caused by **very high expectations** of the person. It seems like perfectionism is real and they have a goal to be this perfect imaginary person.

For example: maybe they want to be a perfect mom, or look perfect, or have a perfect house and family, etc. It is like **perfectionism is an idol in their mindset.** A stronghold and a determined goal how they should look and be.

Their **mind is set on unrealistic expectations** and this causes a lot of stress to them and people around them.

People close to them sometimes feel inferior and pressured to be up to standard. Spouses suffer because they feel like slobs or lazy in the presence of this person.

Anxiety causes a fight or flight response in the body. Every organ works harder due to higher awareness and possibly causing "adrenal fatigue" or chronic fatigue.

The constant readiness to respond to one's environment and release of adrenaline from adrenal glands can lead to **all kinds of fatigue and aches.**

CHAPTER 6

AMPLIFIED SADNESS

For every crime, there is a period of jail time. For stealing a vehicle, you may go to jail for one year.

Once you served your sentence for a particular crime, you are free. The door opens and you can go.

Most people with depression sit in a jail with an open door. THEY HAVE DONE THEIR TIME. They suffered enough.

Many depressed people smile immediately when I tell them they did their time. I see this beautiful smile come instantly on a very depressed face, realizing it is the truth.

You suffered enough. You did your time for the crime!

The door of the jail is open. GO!

Practical Points

- Look for **guilt and shame.** Depression comes because **someone accused and judged them.** You need an accuser to accuse, and a judge to sentence them.

- People sometimes **do this to themselves.** They feel inadequate as a husband, wife, at work, or as a mother.

- A traumatic event as a young child could bring on shame or guilt. They turn on themselves and **reject or self-destruct** by judging.

Psalms 69:20

"Reproach has **broken my heart**, and I am full of **heaviness**; I looked for someone to take pity, but there was none;

And for comforters, but I found none."

- Reproach means **shame** and heaviness indicates **sadness like depression.**

CHAPTER 7

DOOR-OPENING SPIRITS

In the book of Job, Satan complained he could not touch Job, because God had a **protecting hedge** around him.

When we **live in peace,** I believe that spiritual protection is the same as we read in Job.

BUT when a **traumatic event** in our life happens, like abuse or the breakup of a marriage, door-opening spirits come.

They damage that protective "hedge" around us. They open a door to other spirits. Spirits like anxiety can open a door to sickness. Somehow **trauma** happened **that open a door to a severe anxiety.** Other door-opening spirits is bitterness, disappointment, self-hatred, self-rejection and unforgiveness.

Practical points

- Look for the door opening spirits, by **DECLARING** over the **oppressed person,** "I close the door of bitterness, unforgiveness, jealousy, offence, etc."

CHAPTER 8

WHAT DO WE DO WITH THE ATMOSPHERE?

Intercessors are precious! They are like precious stones set in a golden crown of a king.

Intercessors come in and literally rip open the heaven above us. They pray very loud with **bold declarations** exalting the Lord and His Kingdom.

Suddenly we are in the **atmosphere of His Presence.**

Matthew 11:12

"And from the days of John the Baptist until now the kingdom of heaven suffers violence, **and the violent take it by force.**"

Once the atmosphere of **His Presence is tangible** - WHAT DO WE DO WITH IT?

Practical points

- The intercessors bring in the atmosphere of heaven. **Now like a king** in a kingdom, **make your declarations** so that **you can see** the POWER and goodness of God.

CHAPTER 9

IN THE ATMOSPHERE THE KING REIGNS.

The Kingdom of God **reacts on your declarations**. It is important to know that in the atmosphere, **you step out** and do some bold declarations.

Job 22:28

"**You will also declare** a thing, and **it will be established** for you; so light will shine on your ways."

Practical points

- After worship in church on Sundays, it is a good place to start. The church sang and worshipped beautifully and the Lord is pleased.

- Now it is time to step out and make some declarations. **Test the "power of the atmosphere."**

- Pray for someone close to you for healing and see if **the atmosphere carries your words.**

- Like a king, make declarations like "Precious Holy Spirit, **come and touch this person**" or if praying for someone for healing, say, "**I close the door** of self-destruction, anxiety, self-rejection, unforgiving."

CHAPTER 10

YOU ARE ESTABLISHED

In God's kingdom angels left a position that was given to them. **They were established** in a position **to keep a place of authority for Him** and so serve Him.

Jude 1:6

"And the angels who **did not keep their proper domain,** but left their own abode, He has reserved in everlasting chains under darkness for the judgment of the great day;"

So you are **established in Christ** with authority and power to do good works for God. **Good works in the spiritual.**

2 Corinthians 1:21-22

"Now He who establishes us with you in Christ and has anointed us is God."

Practical Points

- Note that **you are anointed in Christ.** I love the word established because you can see **we are placed in a position of authority.** We are anointed and positioned by God.

CHAPTER 11

LET'S TALK ABOUT THE OIL

Shepherds used olive oil to rub on the head of their sheep **for protection** from insects. This kept insects away from the ears of the sheep and prevented infection.

So, the rubbing of olive oil on sheep became traditionally and symbolic of protection, healing and blessing.

Oil was poured out over people as a **sign of empowerment and authority.** Prophet Samuel was told by God to anoint David as King.

Practical Points

- Understanding the anointing is **extremely important** for ministering to people. **Be anointed with the Holy Spirit and His power. (To walk in the Spirit is a daily choice.)**

Acts 10:38

"How God anointed Jesus of Nazareth with the Holy Spirit and with power, who went about doing good and healing all who were oppressed by the devil, for God was with Him."

CHAPTER 12

WHAT IS IN THE OIL?

For **effective ministry, you need three ingredients** in the oil. You need the **Holy Spirit and power.** Jesus was anointed with these two.

But **you get the oil with three ingredients,** namely Jesus (The Word of God), the Holy Spirit, and Power.

Acts 10:38

"How **God anointed** Jesus of Nazareth **with** the Holy Spirit and with power, who went about doing well and **healing all** who were oppressed by the devil, for God was with Him."

Practical Points

- The Word of God is **anointed**. The anointing came because God **wanted Jesus to do well**. God wanted him to heal **all who were oppressed by the devil.**

- **The anointing is for service.** Lucifer was **the author of all** sickness and oppression, now known as Satan.

CHAPTER 13

THE ANOINTING IS FOR OBEDIENCE

To minister to people without the anointing is to mow your lawn with a **bladeless lawnmower**. Not to show people the **demonstrations of the Spirit and power** opens the door for human and demonic doctrine.

Hebrews 2:4

"God also **bearing witness** both with **signs** and **wonders**, with **various miracles**, and **gifts of the Holy Spirit**, according to His own will."

Practical points

- Be anointed! **Obedience attracts the oil** on your life. Walk with anointed people. The anointing that is on them **will rub off on you.**

- Elisha followed Prophet Elijah till he got the power and Holy Spirit that was on him. He noticed that Elijah **used the anointing to serve God** and His people Israel. The anointing **comes by obedience and for service.**

- Be anointed. **Make sure you are anointed.** Demonstrations of the Holy Spirit and Power **is God** bearing witness of the **True Gospel.**

CHAPTER 14

THE BROKEN HEART

Many people suffer from a broken heart. Circumstances in that person's life caused a lot of trauma and hurt that broke their heart.

John 10:10

"**The thief** does not come except to **steal, and to kill, and to destroy.** I have come that they may have life, and that they may have it more abundantly."

Spirits can use people to break your heart. They **live their desires through people** and use people to come against you.

Many families got hurt though **spirits of alcohol and drug addiction.** Children suffered from sexual abuse due to **a sexual spirit in the offender.** Fathers and mothers with **spirits of anger** in them, end up with physical abuse toward their loved ones.

Practical points

- **The Truth reveals to us that we have an enemy.** This enemy has an **end point of killing**. He steals, destroys and oppresses.

CHAPTER 15

THE BROKEN HEART IS AN OPEN DOOR

You can call it **soul wounds**, but a broken heart is an open door to **many physical and emotional problems.**

I believe spirits that cause pain, sickness and disease come in through a broken heart. **The broken heart is an open door.** It is like that hedge God put around Job, and Satan noted he could not touch Job because of that protection.

Proverbs 17:22

"A merry heart does good, like medicine, **but a broken spirit dries the bones.**"

Practical points

- **People with skeletal pain** like back pain, etc., **look for a broken heart. Command every spirit of infirmity** or any other spirits **to come out.** You will be amazed by the results.

- The anointing is to heal the broken heart.

Isaiah 61:1

"**The Spirit of the Lord God is upon me, because** the Lord has **anointed me** to preach good tidings to the poor; He has sent me to **heal the brokenhearted.**

To proclaim liberty to the captives, and the opening of the prison to those who are bound."

- See, look at Isaiah 61 verse 1 and **you will SEE** that the **anointing power comes for healing the broken heart**.

- Spirits that come through a broken heart **torment with pain**. Spirits of unforgiveness, bitterness, grief, hurt and deep hurt, etc.

- ALSO see **the Spirit is upon you because of the oil of obedience**. AS you heal people and cast out evil spirits **you are obeying the commands of Jesus Christ** and his anointing oil is coming on you. Christ is your **cornerstone**. He healed many and cast out many demons.

- Demons know **who has authority** over them. Anointing is about obedience, service to the Lord, power, and identity in Christ.

CHAPTER 16

THE OIL THAT TEACHES

Spiritual things are taught by the Holy Spirit.

1 John 2:27

"But the anointing which you have received from Him **abides in you,** and you do not need that anyone teach you; but as the same **anointing teaches you** concerning **all things,** and is true, and is not a lie, and just as it has taught you, **you will abide in Him."**

As you minister with the Helper, The Holy Spirit, you will become aware of **spiritual things**.

You will become aware of **His personality and his nature.** The reward of being born again of the Spirit is that you **now can see the Kingdom of God** and can enter it. (see John chapter 3)

Practical points

- The fun part is to **minister with the Holy Spirit**. Especially when you lay your hands on people and **make declarations for healing and deliverance.**

- You know the Holy Spirit **is faithful to your words** and reacts on what you say to that person receiving ministry.

Every time you minister you see a new movement of Him and a new revelation comes. Born again of the Spirit means **you are aware of Spirit all the time.**

- You are **persistent** till **you see Him manifest as the LIVING GOD.** We can have so much of this LIVING GOD, **but we stop short of His manifestations** because we don't know how much we can have of Him.

As the deer pants for the water brooks, So **pants my soul** for You, O God. My soul thirsts for God, for the **living God.** (Psalm 42:1-2)

CHAPTER 17

YOUR MEDITATION BRINGS THE GLORY

Psalms 1:1-2

"Blessed is the man... But his delight is in the law of the Lord, and in His law he meditates day and night."

Meditation brings revelation, and revelation brings manifestation. Seeking the Lord will bring in His Presence, but **when Moses TABERNACLED** with God in his tent, **His visible Glory manifested.**

Exodus 40:35

"And Moses was not able to enter the tabernacle of meeting, because the cloud rested above it, and the **glory of the Lord filled the tabernacle."**

Seeking the Lord will bring in his Presence, but when we tabernacle with the Lord, that will bring in his Glory.

His Glory is known as the Shekinah – **which means HIS abiding Presence.**

Practical Points

- **Meditation on His Word brings revelation.** Revelation brings **manifestation.**

- Blessings come from meditation according to Psalm 1.

- The meditation that is day and night on things of the Word, blesses you. **Blessed is the man that meditates!**

- REVEALED TRUTH for seasons of advancements of spiritual growth.

- **Meditation on the Word** pleases the Lord. **It bears fruit in its season.**

Psalms 1:3

"He shall **be like a tree Planted by the rivers of water**, that brings **forth its fruit in its season**, whose leaf also shall not wither; and **whatever he does shall prosper.**"

CHAPTER 18

GLORY

Glory is usually carried by and on angels. When the shepherds were told about Jesus's birth, the sky was bright because of the Glory on them.

Ezekiel saw the Glory and **the brightness** of it in the temple. He then saw the Glory leaving and getting on the Cherubim. **The cherubim and angels are the taxi[1] of the Glory. (2 Samuel 22:11)**

Ezekiel 10:4

"Then the glory of the Lord went up from the cherub, and paused over the threshold of the temple; and the house was filled with the cloud, and the **court was full of the brightness of the Lord's glory.**"

Glory is also on our heads as a **crown.**

Psalms 8:4-5

"What is man that you are mindful of him, and the son of man that you visit him? For you have made him a little lower than the angels, and **You have crowned him with glory and honor.**"

Practical points

- Glory is far above all the heavens **but the earth shall be filled with it.**

- **Glory gets taxied by angels and cherubim.** Glory is as a crown on your head to honor you and give you spiritual authority.

- Glory is **carried by us and angels.** Jesus desired a **kind of Glory He had with the Father before the creation of the earth.**

- **He** rode upon a cherub, **and flew; and He was seen upon the** wings of the wind. (2 Samuel 22:11 (NJV))

- **Glory is carried by the Hosts of heaven.** That is why it is described in the Bible. **He is the Lord of Hosts.**

- **Angels and we are hosts of the Father's Glory.**[2] (Compare with Ephesians 6:12 where it is noted about **spiritual hosts of wickedness** in heavenly places. The enemy always copy the spiritual things of GOD.)

- Glory shines very bright and is light.

- Glory is God the Father.

CHAPTER 19

SIGNS IN THE GLORY

God said to Noah, He puts the sign in the cloud.

Genesis 9:13

"I set **my rainbow in the cloud,** and it shall be for the **sign** of the covenant between me and the earth."

When God (GLORY) shows up, there are signs and wonders.

Even Nicodemus that visited Jesus at night said that God (GLORY) must be with Jesus because of the signs Jesus did.

Glory through the Bible **is revealed by signs and wonders**. When signs, wonders and miracles show up, **know that Glory is in the room.**

Practical points

- Moses was **in the** Glory cloud[1] **on Mount Sinai** meeting with God.

- **Gold** manifests on people as a sign of His visible Glory (Known as the Golden Glory[2] or **Shekinah**[3] **Glory)**

- This is a sign of the **Cloud of Glory.**

- **Glory** is the abiding or visible weighty Presence of God.

CHAPTER 20

WHAT HAPPENS IN THE CLOUD?

One day as I was ministering to a person, suddenly I saw small particles of gold on her.

This **sign kept following us.**[1] More and more people got blessed with it.

Gold is a sign of the Glory. It is like when you drive to a town, **the road sign** will tell you how far you are from the town.

Coughing and yawning are **signs of the Deliverance realm.**

So, when you see gold on people you know you are in

His **"cloud of Glory.** [2] **"**

1Corinthians 10:1-4

"Moreover, brethren, I do not want you to be unaware that **all our fathers were under the clou**d, all passed through the sea, all were baptized into Moses **in the cloud** and in the sea, **all ate the same spiritual food,** and all drank the same **spiritual drink.** For **they drank of that spiritual Rock** that **followed them**, and that Rock was Christ."

CHAPTER 21

SIGNS OF THE CLOUD

When I see gold on one person, **I then know by scripture** that **all** of Israel were in the cloud. I then look at other people surrounding this person, and it amazes me how the Glory (Gold) gets on everyone around.

Practical points

The manifestation of Gold on people is a sign of the Glory.

Look in the Old Testament how His **Glory** manifested **signs and wonders**.

This sign "preaches" to you that cloud is here.

Now you must have revelation that God is pleased and he crowned you now with His Glory

He crowned you with His goodness and authority.

Psalms 8:4-6

"What is man that you are mindful of him, and the son of man that you visit him? For you have made him a little lower than the angels, and you have **crowned him with glory** and honor.

You have made him to have dominion over the works of your hands; **you have put all things under his feet."**

CHAPTER 22

DECLARATIONS AND HEALING IN THE CLOUD

Israel was in the Glory of God. Can you imagine the number of angels around that were bringing in the LORD of HOSTS?

Deuteronomy 29:5

"**And I have led you** forty years in the wilderness. **Your clothes have not worn out** on you, and your sandals have not worn out on your feet."

Practical Points

- Glory is on angels and us.
- Clothes and sandals have **not worn out for forty years.**
- Wonders are in the Glory.
- Glory was the cloud in the tabernacle[1].
- Glory is the **realm for declarations!**

CHAPTER 23

FROM ANOINTING TO GLORY

It is God's intention to see Him[1]. When we see HIM, WE SEE HIS Glory. His goodness is His glory.

Glory is who God is. We see the Glory on the angels as they tell the shepherds about Jesus being born in Bethlehem. The whole sky lights up as the glory on the angels provide light.

God is convinced that when you see His goodness that

this will raise praise to Jesus Christ. Anointing comes when we serve Jesus Christ.

Anointing is on the Word of GOD. Anointing is the Holy Spirit and power that rests on the Word of God. **The Word of God is Jesus Christ.**

Acts 10:38 indicates that Jesus **functioned in the anointing by doing good works** and healing **all** who was oppressed by the devil. **So, you want the anointing?** Have a revelation of serving the Lord as He served His Father.

If you want the anointing power, have a revelation of serving the Lord as He served His Father. THE ANOINTING IS ABOUT **OBEDIENCE AND SERVING.**

CHAPTER 24

ANOINTING IS THE REALM OF OBEDIENCE

Jesus **teaches his disciples** how to heal and cast out demons. He teaches them it is better to serve.

He tells them that **their faith will increase as they serve.** They ask Him to increase their faith.

His answer to them was **to serve.**

Matthew 10:7-8

"And as you go, preach, saying, 'the kingdom of heaven is at hand.' **Heal** the sick, **cleanse** the lepers, and **raise** the dead, **cast out** demons. Freely you have received, **freely give."**

The same thing happened to the **servant Stephan** that **served and saw the glory of GOD.** While they stoned him, he was looking up to heaven and **saw** Jesus and the **Glory of God.** He was just cleaning and serving tables but then also **serving with the anointing** by healing and doing miracles.

In serving he saw the glory of God and was stoned by religious leaders. (Acts 6)

CHAPTER 25

SERVING WITH THE ANOINTING

Serving with the anointing is the key. Serving with the Holy Spirit and power understands the anointing.

Jesus did not send his disciples without teaching how to heal and how to cast out demons. **He had to connect them with the anointing** and teach them **how to operate with the anointing.**

Seek a person that is anointed in ministry that knows how to advance the Kingdom of God with the anointing. **Elisha had to follow Elijah till he got the power and it was given to him on the mantle[1] of Elijah.**

Now, were there emotions or feelings on that mantle? No. **You can't wait on your feelings and emotions to re- lease the power of the anointing.**

For you to function with His Power, **become a contact point for Him.** If a piece of cloth could serve as a carrier of His power, **how much would He use you?**

CHAPTER 26

FROM THE ANOINTING TO SEEING THE GLORY

The disciples were looking for HELPERS (servants) that can serve at the tables of people. So, they can spend more time in ministry.

Stephan was chosen to serve people at tables.

Acts 6:2

"Then the twelve summoned the multitude of the disciples and said, 'It is not desirable that we should leave the word of God and serve tables.'"

Obviously Stephen was **a man that served WITH the anointing:**

Acts 6:8

And Stephen, **full of faith and power**, did **great wonders and signs** among the people.

Serving with the anointing lead that Stephen saw the **GLORY of God**[1]. Just like Moses saw the GLORY **and got a sign and wonder - A RADIANT FACE.**

CHAPTER 27

WHAT YOU SEE IN THE WORD IS YOURS

Imagination is powerful and spiritual. We like daydreaming and it is like having your own little private cinema in your head. You can think of the past or dream and long for things in the future.

God wants to make sure YOUR SEEING is tuned in like a TV station. He wants you to see Him in the Word. **Make sure your seeing is tuned in on the Word.**

Jeremiah 1:11-12

"Moreover the **word of the Lord** came to me, saying, Jeremiah, **what do you see?** And I said, I see a branch of an almond tree. Then the Lord said to me, **You have seen well, for I am ready to perform My word.**"

Practical points

- Meditation on His Word is to tabernacle with Him.

- Moses saw His Glory when He tabernacle with Him.

- Moses **spend time with God** in his own tent and called it the tabernacle. **Moses used his own tent**

first[1]. He also saw the glory of God above the mercy seat.

Looking at the Word when ministering to people is to tabernacle with Jesus Christ.

CHAPTER 28

SPIRITS REACT ON GOD'S WILL FOR YOU

The perfect will of **God is the declaration of His Word over you.**

Declaring the Word over a person causes the Holy Spirit to perform Gods Word[1]. You may see **a Holy Spirit "manifestation"** as the **Holy Spirit obediently performs God's perfected will.**

So also, evil spirits will react when God's perfect will is declared over a person. Where the Holy Spirit loves God's Word, the unclean spirits get irritated by it and leave with or without manifestation.

The whole Kingdom of God is in the declaration of His Word. His whole Kingdom is backing up His word that comes forth in **a declaration by us.**

Practical Points:

- Declare HIS WORD over a person, **and wait to see the reaction of the spiritual world.**

- Evil spirits do not like that and want to leave.

The Holy Spirit **loves that and brings healing.**

CHAPTER 29

ANXIETY IN MINISTRY: "TIMOTHY SYNDROME"

Fear comes against the release of God's power. It comes against our anointing. It comes against your boldness. **Christ is your boldness.**

Fear and anxiety **prevent you from being effective.**

Confidence in God **overcomes** fear. **BUT GOD's secret weapon against fear is the anointing.**

When we try to please people, our focus is then on people and **departs from the things of the Spirit.**

As in any ministry and working with people, opinions can hurt your feelings. Sometime people mean well and can do a lot of damage with their words.

Some people can be bluntly rude and angry and hurt very sensitive people of God.

Timothy was a "spiritual son" of Apostle Paul.

I believe Timothy **was controlled and intimidated by his congregation.** He suffered from anxiety **and this affected his ability to minister effectively.**

How would he lead and overcome such domination, intimidation, and control from his congregation?

2 Timothy 1:7

"For God has not **given us a spirit** of fear, **but of power** and of love and of a sound mind."

He was young and inexperienced in ministry. Timothy was a leader of a church in Ephesus. **He had a fear for men and people.**

Apostle Paul gave Timothy the solution. Paul advised him **to serve with the anointing.** The **anointing overcomes** every human spirit and opinion. Keep ministering **with the power of the Holy Spirit.**

Timothy 1:6 (ESV)

"For this reason I remind you to **fan into flame the gift of God**, which is in you through the **laying on** of my **hands**."

Practical Points

- **The anointing cannot be controlled.** Serve with the anointing and you will be like Samson.

- Every time Samson was bound, the Holy Spirit and power ripped him lose.

- No human opinion or anything religious can bind the anointing. **Be faithful to the manifestations of the anointing,** and you will have no congregation or member able to control, intimidate, and dominate you.

- The spirit of fear and trauma from past words spoken over you will leave **as the anointing honors you, because you honor the anointing.**

- **Confidence will return as people will see the demonstrations of the Holy Spirit is with you**[1]. **Do not neglect** the **demonstrations of the Holy Spirit**. Do not lose your focus of the **things of the Spirit.**

1 John 2:27

"But the anointing which you have received from Him **abides in you,** and you do not need that anyone teach you; but as the **same anointing teaches you concerning all things,** and is true, and is not a lie, and just as it has taught you, **you will abide in Him.**"

"FAN INTO FLAME THE ANOINTING!!"

CHAPTER 30

KNOW YOUR KINGDOMS (KINGDOM OF HEAVEN)

David was the King of Israel. The kings that reigned after him were mostly a failure. The sin of the Kings was the cause for Israel to be exiled to Babylon. But God is bringing Jesus Christ back to Jerusalem to sit on the throne of King David.

This will be a kingdom in the flesh. The Bible talks about the millennium.

The **kingdom of heaven** is currently run by mostly men and churches. Flesh and blood inherit the king **kingdom of heaven.** It has tolerance for every kind of doctrine, man's opinion, demonic doctrine, etc.

The **kingdom of heaven** has tolerance!

Romans 2:4

"Or do you despise the riches of His goodness, forbearance, and longsuffering, not knowing that the goodness of God leads you to repentance?"

CHAPTER 31

KNOW YOUR KINGDOMS (KINGDOM **OF GOD**)

Matthew 6:33

"But seek first the **kingdom of God** and His righteousness, and all these things shall be added to you."

The **kingdom of God** has NO tolerance. When it comes in it causes manifestations, it is **a spiritual kingdom** and flesh and blood cannot inherit it.

1 Corinthians 15:50

"Now this I say, brethren, that flesh and blood cannot inherit the **kingdom of God;** nor does corruption inherit incorruption."

The **kingdom of God** is connected with the **anointing:**

Matthew 12:28

"But if I cast out demons by the Spirit of God, surely the **kingdom of God** has come upon you."

The **kingdom of heaven** without the **kingdom of God** is like a lawnmower without a blade. All noise but now spiritual progress.

CHAPTER 32

JESUS HANDS OVER THE KINGDOM OF HEAVEN TO THE FATHER

1 Corinthians 15:24

"Then comes the end, when He delivers the **kingdom to God** the Father, when He puts an end to all rule and all authority and power."

1 Corinthians 15:28

Now when all things are made subject to Him, then the Son Himself will also be subject to Him who put all things under Him that God may be all in all.

Jesus talks **about two kingdoms,** but it is one kingdom. One is **flesh and spiritual (the kingdom of heaven),** the other one **is only spiritual (the kingdom of God),** the one has tolerance and can be perverted; the other one has no tolerance and causes spiritual manifestations.

Matthew 19:23-24

"Then Jesus said to His disciples, 'Assuredly, I say to you that it is hard for a rich man to enter the **kingdom of heaven.** And again I say to you, it is easier for a camel to go through the eye of a needle than for a rich man to enter **the kingdom of God.'"**

CHAPTER 33

THE KINGDOM OF GOD IS SPIRITUAL AND HAS MANIFESTATIONS

John 3:2

"This man came to Jesus by night and said to Him, 'Rabbi, we know that **You are a teacher come from God;** for no one can do these signs that You do **unless God is with him.'"**

Jesus tells him that **no man** can **see the kingdom of God or enter it**. Because it is **spiritual.**

John 3:5-6

"Jesus answered, 'Most assuredly, I say to you, unless one is **born of water and the Spirit,** he cannot enter the kingdom of God. That which is born of the flesh is flesh, and that which is **born of the Spirit is spirit.'"**

Jesus was telling Nicodemus a secret. The kingdom of God **can only be seen if you are aware of the things of the Holy Spirit.**

When you **desire to see the "living God",** your soul must pant for Him like the soul of the writer of Psalms 42:2 did.

Psalm 42:2

"My soul thirsts for God, for the living God. When shall I come and appear before God?"

FINAL PRACTICAL COMMENTS

- Spirits love to manifest.

- The Holy Spirit **manifest life** and the enemy death (according to Jesus in John 10:10)

- It is important for you to have the desire like the author of Psalm 42:2. His soul **desired God as the "living God."**

Psalms 42:1-2

"As the deer pants for the water brooks, so pants my soul for You, O God."

My soul thirsts for God, for the living God. When shall I come and appear before God?

- **Love and seek God till He manifests as the "living God." (this is the key)**

- Walk with and learn from **truly anointed mentors.** The **oil of obedience to Jesus Christ** will come upon your life and empower you - this is called the anointing, and it is for service to the Lord. The anointing is the realm of obedience, authority, empowerment, identity in Christ, sonship.

- The anointing is the realm of obedience, authority, empowerment, identity in Christ, and sonship.

- Understand the PURPOSE of the anointing.

- Meditate on Isaiah 61 about the purpose of the anointing.

- Anointing is for obedience and SERVICE to our Lord Jesus Christ.

- The anointing is **the oil of obedience**.

- It is **the empowerment** of obedience to Christ.

- It is for advancing **the kingdom of God** here on **earth. (the kingdom of heaven)**

- It is authority.

- It is for **spiritual good works** Acts 10:38

- It is the commandments to disciples of Jesus Christ (Matthew 10:7-8)

- **By ministering with the anointing** (Holy Spirit and Power) you will start seeing His Glory.

- Glory is God himself.

- The realm of Glory **is in seeing God in the Word.**

- Meditation on God's Word is **time spend with God.**

- Seeing God's Word is seeing His Glory.

John 11:40

"Jesus said to her, 'Did I not say to you that if you would believe **you would see the glory of God?'"**

ANOINTING

1 John 2:27 (NKJV)

But the **anointing** which you have received from Him abides in you, and you do not need that anyone teach you; but as the same **anointing** teaches you concerning all things, and is true, and is not a lie, and just as it has taught you, you will abide in Him.

Acts 10:38 (NKJV)

How God **anointed** Jesus of Nazareth with the Holy Spirit and with power, who went about doing good and healing all who were oppressed by the devil, for God was with Him.

Isaiah 61 (NKJV)

"The Spirit of the Lord GOD *is* upon Me,
Because the LORD has **anointed** Me
To preach good tidings to the poor;
He has sent Me to heal the brokenhearted,
To proclaim liberty to the captives,
And the opening of the prison to *those who are bound*

1 Samuel 16:13 (NKJV)

Then Samuel took the horn of oil and **anointed** him in the midst of his brothers; and the Spirit of the LORD came upon David from that day forward. So Samuel arose and went to Ramah.

POWER

Acts 1:8 (NKJV)

But you shall receive **power** when the Holy Spirit has come upon you; and you shall be witnesses to Me in Jerusalem, and in all Judea and Samaria, and to the end of the earth.

2 Timothy 1:7 (NKJV)

For God has not given us a spirit of fear, but of **power** and of love and of a sound mind.

Habakkuk 3:4 (NKJV)

His brightness was like the light;
He had rays *flashing* from His hand,
And there His **power** *was* hidden.

About the Author

Dr. Rudi is an ordained minister, author and physician. He is focused on demonstrating the love of Christ Jesus for people by advancing the Kingdom of God with signs, wonders and miracles.

He loves the anointing of the Holy Spirit and has a passion for healing, deliverance and glory ministry.

Dr Rudi is also the leader of Healing and Deliverance Rooms of Sylvan Lake Alberta in Canada since 2014. (Frontline Worship Centre Sylvan Lake) doctorrudi.com

The scriptures declare that signs, wonders and miracles will accompany those who simply believe. I have known Dr. Niemand for a number of years and have witnessed the gifts of the Spirit in operation while the character of Christ within serves as fuel fanning the flames of breakthrough. Heaven stands ready to release new realms of HIS glory and sons and daughters are arising and taking their rightful position as the end of the age approaches. The book brings empowerment and propels believers into an enhanced view of their own destiny. Normal Christianity is never naturally normal but supernaturally charged. This is the message. - **Apostle Peter Nash**

"I have known Dr. Rudi for many years and have seen his passion for both Presence and Power! I believe his commitment to teaching and demonstrating the Kingdom is why he sees so many miracles and deliverance." - Todd Bentley

More information: doctorrudi.com

WEBSITE OF DR RUDI

School of Glory and Anointing: doctorrudi.com

Books written by Dr Rudi - available on his website at doctorrudi.com

- Spiritual Power the Crown of a King

- Spiritual Freedom from Anxiety and Depression

Also available on Amazon books and kindle

https://www.amazon.ca/dp/1720374341/ref=cm_sw_r_oth_tai_i_3UKcBbDYAWK21

Order his Book for Bible Study Groups:

Spiritual Freedom from Anxiety and Depression 2018 by Dr Rudi

Order now from this website: doctorrudi.com

NOTES

CHAPTER 1

רוח (*RU.ACH*) 'SPIRIT' (H7307) MEANING

WIND, BREATH, MIND, SPIRIT

https://www.stepbible.org/?q=version=KJV|reference=Gen.1

CHAPTER 17

The word shekinah means, "to be seen," or "a visible manifestation of the divine presence." http://www.newwineinternational.org/writings/view/47-Experiencing-the-Glory-of-God

Joshua Mills Ministries

CHAPTER 18

1. **2 Samuel 22:11 (NKJV) He rode upon a cherub, and flew;And He was seen upon the wings of the wind.**

2. John 17:5 (NKJV) And now, O Father, glorify Me together with Yourself, **with the glory which I had with You before the world was.**

CHAPTER 19

- **Exodus 19:9 (NKJV)** And the LORD said to Moses, "Behold, I come to you in the thick cloud, that the people may hear when I speak with you, and believe you forever."

  So Moses told the words of the people to the LORD.

1. Ruth Ward Heflin, *Glory, Experiencing the Atmosphere of Heaven* (McDouglas Publishing 1990)

2. The word shekinah means, "to be seen," or "a visible manifestation of the divine presence." http://www.newwineinternational.org/writings/view/47-Experiencing-the-Glory-of-God

CHAPTER 20

1. **Mark 16:17 And these signs will follow** those who believe: In My name they will cast out

demons; they will speak with new tongues; **18** they will take up serpents; and if they drink anything deadly, it will by no means hurt them; they will lay hands on the sick, and they will recover."

2. Hebrews 12:1 (NKJV) Therefore we also, **since we are surrounded by so great a cloud** of witnesses, let us lay aside every weight, and the sin which so easily ensnares *us,* and let us run with endurance the race that is set before us,

CHAPTER 22

1. **Tabernacle Glory** was seen when God came to the tent of Moses. The tent was a dwelling place for Moses. It was a covering and a place of rest in the warm desert.

CHAPTER 23

1. **Number 14:21 (ESV)** But truly, as I live, and as all **the earth shall be filled with the glory** of the LORD,

CHAPTER 25

1. 2 Kings 2:8 (NKJV) Now Elijah took his mantle, rolled *it* up, and struck the water; and it was divided this way and that, so that the two of them crossed over on dry ground.

Chapter 26

1. **Numbers 14:21** but truly, as I live, **all the earth shall be filled** with the **glory of the Lord— 22** because all these men **who have seen My glory and the signs which I did in Egypt** and in the wilderness, and have put Me to the test now these ten times, and have not heeded My voice,

Chapter 27

1. Exodus 14:7 (NKJV) **Moses took his tent** and pitched it outside the camp, far from the camp, and called it the tabernacle of meeting. And it came to pass *that* everyone who sought the Lord went out to the tabernacle of meeting which *was* outside the camp.

Chapter 28

1. Jeremiah 1:12 (NKJV)Then the Lord said to me, **"You have seen well, for I am ready to perform My word."**

Chapter 29

1. 2 Kings 2:15 (NKJV) Now when the sons of the prophets who *were* from Jericho saw him, they said, "The spirit of Elijah rests on Elisha." **And they came to meet him, and bowed to the ground before him.**

CHAPTER 30

Dake Study Bible Notes by Rev. Finis Jennings Dake (Dake Publishing, Inc.)

Inspired by following books and resources:

Charles Frances Hunter, How to heal the sick (Whitaker House 1981)

Charles Capps, The Tongue – a creative force (Harrison House 1995)

Dake Study Bible Notes by Rev. Finis Jennings Dake (Dake Publishing, Inc.)

David Herzog, Mysteries of the Glory Unveiled (Destiny Image Publishers 2000)

Derek Prince, Entering the Presence of God (Whitaker House 2007)

Derek Prince, They Shall Expel Demons (1998 published by chosenbooks.com)

Frank and Ida Mae Hammond, Pigs in the Parlour (Impact Christian Books 1973)

H. A. Maxwell Whyte, Demons & Deliverance (Whitaker House 1989)

Inspired by audio CD teachings from Benny Hinn (Toronto - Training for Ministry Conference 2006)

Jack Hayford, Manifest Presence (Chosenbooks 2005)

John Eckhardt, *Deliverance and Spiritual Warfare Manual* (Charisma House 2014)

John G. Lake, The Complete Collection of His Life Teachings, Robert Lairdon Ministries (Witaker House 1999)

Kenneth E. Hagin, *The Believer's Authority* (copyright 1986 RHEMA Bible Church)

Ruth Ward Heflin, *Glory, Experiencing the Atmosphere of Heaven* (McDouglas Publishing 1990)

Smith Wigglesworth, *The Power of Faith* (Whitaker House 2000)